A Little Guide to
MUSHROOMS

RP Minis®
Hachette Book Group
1290 Avenue of the Americas, New York, NY 10104
www.runningpress.com
@Running_Press

First Edition: March 2023

Published by RP Minis, an imprint of Perseus Books, LLC, a subsidiary of Hachette Book Group, Inc. The RP Minis name and logo is a registered trademark of the Hachette Book Group.

The Hachette Speakers Bureau provides a wide range of authors for speaking events. To find out more, go to www.hachettespeakersbureau.com or call (866) 376-6591.

The publisher is not responsible for websites (or their content) that are not owned by the publisher.

ISBN: 978-0-7624-8137-8

What Is a Mushroom?

Ask just about anyone to draw a mushroom, and they'll likely sketch the classic toadstool: a tan- or red-domed cap—maybe with spots—a stem, and possibly some gills. These are the images of mushrooms many people are exposed to the most. But in reality, mushrooms come in myriad shapes, textures, and sizes, as well as every color of the rainbow. Some are tiny bowls, cups, or spoons fit for faerie feasts. There are species that look like daisy-petaled flowers, discarded citrus peels, miniature birds' nests complete with eggs, and even wrinkled brains and spooky zombie fingers poking from the earth. Some are so small they can hardly be seen with the naked eye, while others are so large they could barely fit in a wheelbarrow.

But what is a mushroom, exactly? Mushrooms are fruiting bodies; much like an apple is the reproductive structure of a tree, a mushroom is the visible reproductive structure of a fungus. Most of a fungus's mass exists largely out of view in the soil, under leaves and logs, embedded in the substrate it is growing in. This hidden portion is made up of an extensive net of thread-like tissue called **mycelium**. Mycelium secretes enzymes for digestion and absorbs water and nutrients for the fungus. It also can connect plants and trees in a mutualistic network much like Mother Nature's internet. In a thriving environment, under ideal conditions, there can be an astounding seven to eight miles of mycelium in one cubic inch of soil.

One of the primary goals of living organisms is to reproduce and ensure the survival of their species. When it is time for fungi to do so, they form mushrooms, which in turn produce **spores** containing the fungal organism's genetic material. This process uses up a tremendous amount of energy and resources, so it must be timed wisely to take advantage of the moist conditions that most mushrooms require to reach reproductive maturity. This is why mushrooms are often found popping up in damp, shady forests and soggy lawns after a rainfall.

Warts

Pileus (cap)

Pores

Teeth

Hymenium (underside)

Lamellae (Gills)

Ring / Skirt

Stipe (stem)

Volva

Not all mushrooms are shaped like the classic toadstool, but those that are have many of the same basic parts.

The cap is called a **pileus** in mycological terms. A mushroom's cap serves as protection, structure, and support for the fertile surface found on the underside. They come in every color imaginable, from subdued to shockingly bright. They can be smaller than the head of a pin or as large as an open umbrella,

pointy like a witch's
hat or concave like
a dish. Their sheen
ranges from dull
and chalky to glossy as

a sports car, and their endlessly diverse
textures run the gamut from dry and
leathery to gooey, slimy, warty, spiky,
and even furry.

The underside of a mushroom's cap,
called the **hymenium** in mycology, is
the fertile surface where spores are pro-
duced. Most people are familiar with

gills, or **lamellae**, the ridges that radiate out from the stem like spokes on a wheel. Gills function to increase the surface area of the hymenium. Other mushroom species have developed different means of maximizing this spore-producing real estate. Some have evolved to have toothy projections, while others have developed long, spore-producing tubes that end in openings called **pores**.

A fungus's goal is not only to produce as many spores as possible but also to ensure they have the best chance of traveling the farthest. A mushroom's stem, or **stipe**, is designed to facilitate spore dispersal by elevating the fertile surface to an optimal height so spores can be distributed on air currents or carried by dining insects, hungry slugs and snails, passing animals, and even humans. Stems also come in every color and texture imaginable. In stature, they can be long and slender or stout and stocky enough to dwarf the cap.

Certain mushrooms have specialized structures. One example is the **universal veil**, an egg-like structure found at or under the soil line that encases and protects the young mushroom when it is first developing. In species of *Amanita*, a portion of the universal veil remains at the base of the mushroom's stem as a bulb or cup-like sac called a **volva**. Immature stinkhorns are also enclosed in a universal veil. Some mushrooms have a **partial veil**—a thin, tissuey, cobwebby, or slimy membranous covering that protects the mushroom's developing gills. After the cap fully expands, this partial veil tissue is often left behind as a ring or pendant skirt-like structure on the stem and sometimes as raised warts or patches on the mushroom's cap.

fig. 1

Amanita rubre   Hong rouge

Ecological Roles of Fungi

Fungi are everywhere—in our lawns and forests, in and on our bodies, and even lurking in that forgotten Tupperware container in the back of the fridge. While some fungi are harmful, the vast majority are beneficial to their environments and serve important ecological roles.

Some fungi act as parasites, infecting their hosts and sickening or even killing them. Common human ailments such as ringworm and athlete's foot are caused by fungi. Parasitic fungi like rusts and mildews regularly cause costly damage to important agricultural crops. Fungi even attack other fungi: *Hypomyces lactifluorum* parasitizes species of *Lactarius* and *Russula*, transforming them into the choice edible known as

the lobster mushroom. Hands down, though, the fungal parasites that infect insects are among the most bizarre: these fungi keep their insect hosts alive but take complete control of their actions, using them as zombie minions to spread their spores for them.

A second group is the decomposers known as saprobes. Decay is an essential part of an ecosystem's natural cycle, and decomposers are nature's recycling crew. They feed on dead organic matter, breaking it down into nutrients that can then be used by other organisms, and life begins anew. Fungi are the only multicellular organisms capable of breaking down lignin, the toughest parts of wood and leaves. Without them, every tree that has ever died would still be lying about, and the earth would be buried under an epic leaf pile.

The third group of fungi enters into mutualistic relationships, called **mycorrhiza**, with plants, including food crops and the trees in our forests. In fact, about 90 percent of land plants rely on partnerships with mycorrhizal fungi. Underground microscopic fungal filaments, called **hyphae**, connect with plant rootlets, forming a symbiotic bond. The plant, then tapped into the massive mycelial network of the fungus, has much greater access to nutrients and water. As part of this ancient bartering system, the fungus receives sugars that the plant produces during photosynthesis, a food the fungus is incapable of making itself. In healthy forests, trees connected via this network, sometimes called the "wood wide web," can even share water and nutrients with each other.

Foraging for Mushrooms

Gathering has been an important part of our survival since prehistoric times. Before agriculture and industry, early humans relied on wild plants and mushrooms for both food and medicine.

Today, foraging is a lucrative form of income in many parts of the world. Some mushrooms such as morels, chanterelles, and porcini are difficult or impossible to cultivate commercially, so they must be hand-gathered from the wild. Truffle hunting is alive and well in France and Italy, where the trade of these highly sought-after mushrooms is big business. European truffles are, ounce for ounce, the most expensive food in the world, fetching thousands of dollars per pound. A two-pound (0.9 kg) white truffle sold for a record $330,000 in 2010.

Foraging can be a rewarding hobby and a great way to get outside and connect with nature. Both for success and for safety, foragers must have a working knowledge of specific ecosystems and the trees that grow in them as well as a keen awareness of weather patterns and seasons. Learning to identify mushrooms with 100 percent certainty is a must, as there are sometimes only subtle differences between delicious edibles and toxic look-alikes. Novice foragers should confirm ID with a mycologist or professional forager because a misidentification could cause severe gastrointestinal distress or worse. The forager's credo, and a good rule to *literally* live by, is "when in doubt, throw it out"—or, better, leave it where you found it.

In many parts of Europe, foraging is a national pastime, with knowledge passed down from generation to generation. In the United States, where foraging is not part of the culture in the same way, foraging and eating wild mushrooms can be a scary prospect. The fear of mushrooms even has a name—mycophobia. Foraging in the States is becoming increasingly popular, though, and with proper education and training, even the beginner forager can identify some edible varieties with ease. Though there is a wealth of information in books and on the internet, those who wish to move beyond the basics should consider taking foraging classes or joining a local mushroom club. Nothing can take the place of hands-on learning with an expert.